DESTINED

FOR

SUCCESS

Marty Delmon

Destined for Success
Marty Delmon

Published by:
RPJ & Company, Inc.
Post Office Box 160243
Altamonte Springs, Florida 32716-0243
Web site: www.rpjandco.com

ISBN-10: 0-9761122-7-2
ISBN-13: 978-0-9761122-7-3

Layout & Design:
RPJ & Company, Inc.
www.rpjandco.com

Cover Image by:
© Galina Barskaya - Fotolia.com

Scripture taken from the New King James Version. Copyright 1979, 1980, 1982 by Thomas Nelson, Inc. Used by permission. All rights reserved.

Printed in the United States of America.
April 2009

Published by:

RPJ & COMPANY, INC.
www.rpjandco.com

Table of Contents

INTRODUCTION

Originally written some time ago for the French reader, the contents of this little book remain potent because the source comes from the Word of God. That's timeless power! No matter when or where one applies Scripture like a sword, it works because it cuts through the debris of lies and tradition and puts to work our only true weapon: what God said.

Arriving on French soil as a missionary straight out of Bible school, appalled at their lack of knowledge of the promises of God and how to obtain them – not only salvation but also healing and prosperity plus the rest of the 7,000 promises – I set out to share the enlightenment I had just obtained. This was my first offering.

I printed 2,000 of these books, in French, and I gave them away. Today, twenty years later, it is not uncommon for people to approach me on the street and say, "Aren't you that lady that wrote that book "Destinée a Réussir"? When I acknowledge that yes, I am, and yes, I did, they shower me with gratitude.

In a socialist country where it has been practically impossible to start a new business because of the heavy burden of taxes and fees a new owner must pay, so many people tell me that, nevertheless, they started their own business by using my book. And it worked! They're successful and continue to have success because they persist in following the principles you will read in these pages.

France is softening now and reducing the penalties for new businesses. However, even with a lighter burden to pay the government, new owners will only find success if they follow these guidelines. Households, families and individuals applying these tenets also succeed. In fact, these truths belong to each individual child of God. Jehovah set up this world; it behooves us to do things His way.

Therefore may you prosper beyond your wildest dreams! Your Heavenly Father wants it that way so He made a way (He's the Waymaker) for you to succeed. He loves your achievement! Follow and continue to follow what He has to say because you are destined for success!

Marty Delmon 1

CHAPTER ONE

DESTINED TO POSSESS RICHES

One day my husband and I took a walk. We decided to stroll in a luxurious shopping mall, a beautiful place full of statues, fountains and sophisticated shops. Hardly anybody was there. In turning a corner we chanced upon an auction installed in the hallway. On a table along the side all sorts of little delicacies, cakes, cookies and chocolate covered strawberries had been arranged for the expected audience. So we helped ourselves, piled some goodies on little plates and sat with the other spectators waiting for the auction to begin.

It turned out to be an elegant fur shop auctioning its coats. The crowd numbered twelve or so people therefore the coats sold at a bargain price. One gorgeous coat valued at $12,000 went for $2,000. At that time in our lives, money was not a problem. We had started to receive the effects of putting into practice the Biblical principles of wealth in finances and money had begun to enter our bank accounts.

While we were sitting there, I turned toward my husband. He was sweating. His eyes bulged out of his head. His face had turned red. I thought to myself, "This man is either going to have a heart attack, or he is going to buy me a fur coat!" We came from very simple backgrounds and I had a difficult time imagining myself owning a fur coat. I put down my little plate of sweets, took his plate from him, set it on a chair, grabbed him by the arm and pulled him out of there! We ran around the corner and had a good laugh at how close I came to owning a fur coat.

I forgot the incident, but one night not long after that as I was doing the dishes the Lord spoke very clearly. He said, **"If I didn't make the fur coats of this world for you, who did I make them for?"** I had a hard time answering that question! Did He make them for worldly people who are not saved? It would seem that way because they're the ones who have them. Didn't God put all the good things on the earth for his own people? Didn't He make abundance for those that He loves and cherishes? Jesus said that He came so that we would have abundant life (John 10:10)! However, when you see who has the riches of the world, it can easily be seen that it is not the people of God! The children of God, the Christians, do not have the abundance.

The people of the world who don't know what to do with money are those who have the riches in their possession. I believe the last thing that Satan wants is for Christians to have money because he knows that if we have the money in our possession we will spend it on the spreading of the Gospel around the world and his game will be over! That's why he works so hard for the money to be in the possession of the people of the world. They will spend it only on themselves and to satisfy their own desires.

We, the Christians, are destined to possess riches. The Bible tells us that we have been created to have all the blessings. We who are born again know that Jesus Christ became poor so that we could become rich. But the perpetual debate asks, "Of what nature are these riches? Are they physical or are they spiritual? Are we concerned with wealth here on earth, or do we wait for heaven to obtain this wealth?"

That is why my subject is money. Should Christians have any? What should they do with it? Is money really the root of all evil? And the only source for the answer to all these questions is the Bible. All other arguments come only from men. From the beginning to the end the Bible speaks of wealth.

Sometimes it is good to go back to the beginning of things. For example, the Lord loves for us to remember our beginnings with Him. In speaking to the Church of Ephesus He said:

REVELATION 2:4
Nevertheless I have this against you, that you have left your first love.

Do you remember how much you loved the Lord at the beginning when you were first born again? Your relationship with Him was better than any romance novel! The Lord wants us to return to that first love.

Sometimes it is necessary to return to the beginning of things in order to better understand what is happening now.

Sometimes it is the only way to see the truth because between the beginning and today men have corrupted the intentions of God for their own purposes. That has happened with money. The original intentions of God were for His people, those who loved Him, believed in Him, walked with Him and served Him, to have the wealth of the world.

PROVERBS 13:22
But the wealth of the sinner is stored up for the righteous.

Man corrupted this intention to the point that today the Body of Christ has been taken captive by a spirit of poverty. That is exactly the opposite of the plan of God! The spirit of poverty produces an impoverished mind, that is to say that poverty rules the thought life. There are a myriad of ways in which the spirit of poverty manifests itself in the thoughts of people. For example, some Christians think that they only need a little bit of money but not enough to provide a level of comfort that would make people jealous. Other Christians feel they need to live by what they call "faith", but in reality this means they barely have enough money to feed themselves! Others decide they are going to get a lot of money, enjoy it, and so they let their Church attendance slide in order to avoid being embarrassed by their riches.

Here is the truth: poverty was Satan's idea. He made poverty out to be attractive and popularized the idea in the Eastern religious thinking. Then he introduced this idea in the Church of God in the fourth century when Constantine nationalized Christianity. Overnight the Roman Empire became "Christian" whether the people were born again or not. As a consequence the people simply brought their own traditions into this new religion. One of their traditions alleged that God wanted people to suffer and to be poor.

Greed is also an idea that comes from Satan, the act of accumulating wealth for strictly personal reasons. There's nothing wrong in acquiring riches, but what is so bad is to do it for egotistical goals. It is doubly tragic to see someone with a poverty mentality full of greed.

Pride is another offshoot of Satan. He persuades people to be proud of the money that they earn. What a ridiculous idea! Money is nothing more than a tool. Tools must be maintained in good condition, but it is illogical to attach pride to them. Does a hairdresser have pride in his scissors? A sculptor in his carving tools? A writer in his computer? A dishwasher in his soap? When Satan's ideas are considered with objectivity, they appear as the lies and deceptions that they really are.

But that's enough about Satan and his works! What does God want for His own? In order to respond to that question, we must go back to the beginning. What were God's intentions concerning prosperity, wealth and money for the man and the woman that he created? These are the first words God proclaimed from His own mouth regarding man:

GENESIS 1:26
Then God said, Let Us make man in Our image, according to Our likeness; let them have dominion over the fish of the sea, over the birds of the air, and over the cattle, over all the earth and over every creeping thing that creeps on the earth.

In reading that, does it seem that God wanted us to only get by? That we have just the minimum of comfort? That we depend on others to feed us and give us clothes? Or that we should be embarrassed by what we possess? NO! A million times no! God made us in His image. He designed us to reign. He destined us for riches. But then Adam fell! Adam sold his dominion to Satan and Satan, instead of Adam, became the prince of this world.

2 CORINTHIANS 4:3, 4
But even if our gospel is veiled, it is veiled to those who are perishing, whose minds the god of this age has blinded, who do not believe, lest the light of the gospel of the glory of Christ, who is the image of God, should shine on them.

The fall of Adam brought death and destruction to the spirit of man. Spiritually, God and man were no longer "connected". Man must be born again, spiritually, in order to be reconnected to God. However, the fall of Adam did not change God. He has always loved His creation and has always wanted to bless His people in whatever manner they would permit Him to do so. God did not stop blessing those who served Him. With the fall of Adam man acquired the knowledge of good and evil, which means that man then had the opportunity to choose between good and evil.

DEUTERONOMY 30:19
I call heaven and earth as witnesses today against you, that I have set before you life and death, blessing and cursing; therefore choose life, that both you and your descendants may live;

There is a distinction in the Old Testament between the sons of man and the sons of God. The sons of man were those who chose to live without the guidance of God. They lived according to their own passions and became evil.

GENESIS 6:5
Then the Lord saw that the wickedness of man was great in the earth, and that every intent of the thoughts of his heart was only evil continually.

The sons of God, however, preserved their relationship with God and lived in a manner that pleased Him.

GENESIS 6:9
Noah was a just man, perfect in his generation. Noah walked with God.

Look at Enoch.

GENESIS 5:24
And Enoch walked with God; and he was not, for God took him.

Each day God and Enoch took a walk together. One day God brought Enoch home for supper and Enoch never came back. Now that's a close relationship! Noah was a just man who found favor in the eyes of the Lord. After the flood it is written:

GENESIS 9:1, 3
So God blessed Noah and his sons, and said to them: "Be fruitful and multiply, and fill the earth. Every moving thing that lives shall be food for you. I have given you all things, even as the green herbs.

God said: **"I have given you all things..."** That seems rather generous, doesn't it? Consider Abram, the man who became Abraham. God said:

GENESIS 12:2, 3
I will make you a great nation; I will bless you and make your name great; and you shall be a blessing. I will bless those who bless you, and I will curse him who curses you; and in you all the families of the earth shall be blessed.

What did that blessing mean in terms of money?

GENESIS 13:2
Abram was very rich in livestock, in silver, and in gold.

Abram and his nephew Lot had to separate from each other because:

GENESIS 13:6
Now the land was not able to support them, that they might dwell together, for their possessions were so great that they could not dwell together.

It does not seem to me that Abram had only a narrow margin of comfort, or that he had been incapable of feeding his family, or that he was embarrassed by his wealth. He took his riches in a good way. He took them as receiving the promise of God! After that the Lord gave a new name to Abram in that he called him Abraham, which means, "father of many nations," and it was said of him:

GENESIS 24:1
Now Abraham was old, well advanced in age; and the Lord had blessed Abraham in all things.

His servant said of him:

GENESIS 24:35
The Lord has blessed my master greatly, and he has become great; and He has given him flocks and herds, silver and gold, male and female servants, and camels and donkeys.

God does not treat His children any differently today. That which He did for His servant Abraham, He will do for His children now, if not more. Doesn't a man treat his son better than he treats a servant? Under the Old Covenant the people of God were called servants. Under the New Covenant the people of God are called His children because the blood of Jesus has been used to adopt us into the family of God.

GALATIANS 4:6, 7
And because you are sons, God has sent forth the Spirit of His Son into your hearts, crying out, "Abba, Father!" Therefore you are no longer a slave but a son, and if a son, then an heir of God through Christ.

At the death of Abraham the Bible tells us:

GENESIS 25:5
And Abraham gave all that he had to Isaac.

But Isaac became even richer than Abraham.

GENESIS 26:12-14
Then Isaac sowed in that land, and reaped in the same year a hundredfold; and the Lord blessed him. The man began to prosper, and continued prospering until he became very prosperous; for he had possessions of flocks and possessions of herds and a great number of servants. So the Philistines envied him.

If the servants of God invoked envy from those who did not serve God because of their great riches, shouldn't the children of God invoke envy from the children of Satan, the unbelievers? The servants of God invoked envy, even when they were in captivity. The people who walked with God continued to prosper even through 430 years of slavery in Egypt.

EXODUS 1:7
But the children of Israel were fruitful and increased abundantly, multiplied and grew exceedingly mighty; and the land was filled with them.

When the time came for Moses to lead the Israelites out of Egypt, God assured their financial riches. He instructed Moses:

EXODUS 11:2
Speak now in the hearing of the people and let every man ask from his neighbor and every woman from her neighbor, articles of silver and articles of gold.

In verse 7 Moses clearly says to Pharaoh:

But against none of the children of Israel shall a dog move its tongue, against man or beast, that you may know that the Lord does make a difference between the Egyptians and Israel.

God makes the same distinction today between His people and the people of the world. He makes the rain to fall and the sun to shine equally on the good and on the bad, but He promises an abundant life to His people, to those who recognize Jesus as Lord and obey His voice.

JOHN 10:10
The thief does not come except to steal, and to kill, and to destroy. I have come that they may have life and that they may have it more abundantly.

ISAIAH 1:19
If you are willing and obedient, you shall eat the good of the land;

When the Israelites left Egypt, they left behind them the shackles of man.

JOHN 8:36
Therefore if the Son makes you free, you shall be free indeed.

The Israelites began their journey toward the Promised Land as rich people.

EXODUS 12:35, 36
Now the children of Israel had done according to the word of Moses and they had asked from the Egyptians articles of silver, articles of gold, and clothing. And the Lord had given the people favor in the sight of the Egyptians, so that they

granted them what they requested. Thus they plundered the Egyptians.

The Presence of the Holy Spirit in our lives is our Promised Land on the earth. It is He who leads us towards wealth. Moses led the Israelites for more than 40 years. Before his death, he gave them final instructions. These instructions are also for us. There is only one difference. The Israelites had a multitude of laws to strictly follow. We have only one: the law of love.

JOHN 13:34
A new commandment I give to you, that you love one another; as I have loved you, that you also love one another.

The easiest manner in which to practice this law of love is to act as if each person that you meet is Jesus in disguise. In fact, that is not a supposition, it is the truth. Each born again person has the Spirit of Jesus in him and each unsaved person has the necessary potential for the Spirit of Jesus to live in him because Jesus died for each of them. When Jesus comes in our heart and we become born again the Bible says that the love of God is poured out in our hearts.

ROMANS 5:5
Now hope does not disappoint because the love of God has been poured out in our hearts by the Holy Spirit who was given to us.

It is like the familiar fairy tale told to children about a certain king. An evil sorcerer cast a spell on him and he was transformed into a vile frog. The only way of breaking that spell was for a pretty princess to kiss him. He finally found one who agreed to kiss him and when she did the spell was broken. The king married her and they lived happily ever after. Maybe it was the Holy Spirit who inspired that story. Satan certainly transforms people into ugly frogs but the love of Jesus makes them become kings!

REVELATION 1:6; 5:10
1:6 And has made us kings and priests to His God and Father, to Him be glory and dominion forever and ever. Amen.
5:10 And have made us kings and priests to our God; and we shall reign on the earth.

He has commanded us to love. We must let the love of God be poured out in our hearts. And if we do this, we receive these blessings:

DEUTERONOMY 28:1-14
1 Now it shall come to pass, if you diligently obey the voice of the Lord your God, to observe carefully all His commandments which I command you today, that the Lord your God will set you high above all nations of the earth.
2 And all these blessings shall come upon you and overtake you, because you obey the voice of the Lord your God:
3 Blessed shall you be in the city, and blessed shall you be in the country.
4 Blessed shall be the fruit of your body, the produce of your ground and the increase of your cattle and the offspring of your flocks.
5 Blessed shall be your basket and your kneading bowl.
6 Blessed shall you be when you come in, and blessed shall you be when you go out.

7 *The Lord will cause your enemies who rise against you to be defeated before your face; they shall come out against you one way and flee before you seven ways.*

8 *The Lord will command the blessing on you in your storehouses and in all to which you set your hand, and He will bless you in the land which the Lord your God is giving you.*

9 *The Lord will establish you as a holy people to Himself, just as He has sworn to you, if you keep the commandments of the Lord your God and walk in His ways.*

10 *Then all peoples of the earth shall see that you are called by the name of the Lord, and they shall be afraid of you.*

11 *And the Lord will grant you plenty of goods, in the fruit of your body, in the increase of your livestock, and in the produce of your ground, in the land of which the Lord swore to your fathers to give you.*

12 *The Lord will open to you His good treasure, the heavens, to give the rain to your land in its season and to bless all the work of your hand. You shall lend to many nations, but you shall not borrow.*

13 *And the Lord will make you the head and not the tail; you shall be above only, and not be beneath, if you heed the commandments of the Lord your God, which I command you today, and are careful to observe them.*

14 *So you shall not turn aside from any of the words which I command you this day, to the right or the left, to go after other gods to serve them.*

After reading this do you think God wants His people to be poor? From the very beginning God wanted us to be rich! He blessed men financially then, and He does the same right now, if we will permit Him to do so. If we will unburden our minds from that poverty mentality and submit ourselves to the plans and purposes of God, He will bless us financially.

Take another look at Verse 8.

8 *The Lord will command the blessing on you in your storehouses....*

One of God's plans and purposes for us is to have personal storehouses. What's a storehouse? To me it is a savings account. To others it could be mutual funds. Some might call it investment property. The Lord knows where to put the money that He wants in a storehouse. Saving is a mandate from God; after all, He promises to bless it and not only bless it but He commands the blessing on your storehouse.

Try it. Try putting some money aside every time you receive money and see what God does for you! Do you live from paycheck to paycheck? Try reducing your spending in order to put some money aside, every month, and see what the Lord will do for you. He believes in saving. With the help of God, most millionaires are just ordinary citizens who saved their way into having a million or so dollars.

It is said that people with a poverty mentality are either so stingy they live in a state of self-inflicted lack, or they are so liberal they spend every dime they've got. Did you know that 80% of college seniors already have credit card debt they can't pay? This is indicative of a poverty mentality. Be daring. Put money aside into a savings account of some kind because God says He will bless it.

We call a poverty mentality "stinkin' thinkin'". That means that these poverty thoughts stink in the nostrils of God. The Bible often speaks of God smelling certain aromas from the earth.

GENESIS 8:21
And the Lord smelled a soothing aroma.

REVELATION 8:4
And the smoke of the incense with the prayers of the saints ascended before God from the angel's hand.

If He can smell our thoughts regarding money it must make Him sick to His stomach! "Stinkin' thinkin'" makes up negative thoughts like: 'Money is hard to come by.' 'I can't make ends meet with what I make.' 'The government takes all my money.' 'I don't see any way out of this financial mess.' 'My family has always been poor.' 'It's not my lot in life to be rich.' 'It's my money and I'll do what I want with it.' 'Don't ask me for money; I have to take care of myself.' 'If I don't take care of myself, who will?'

I believe that one of the hardest thoughts for God to hear is when one of His own children says something like this: 'I don't have much money, but it is sufficient for my position in life.' That must tear His heart because with our new birth we became His children and, as His children, we have the highest position in the world.

EPHESIANS 1:3, 20-21; 2:4-6
1:3 Blessed be the God and Father of our Lord Jesus Christ who has blessed us with every spiritual blessing in the heavenly places in Christ.

20 *which He worked in Christ when He raised Him from the dead and seated Him at His right hand in the heavenly places,*

21 *far above all principality and power and might and dominion, and every name that is named, not only in this age but also in that which is to come.*

2:4 *But God, who is rich in mercy because of His great love with which He loved us,*

5 *even when we were dead in trespasses, made us alive together with Christ (by grace you have been saved),*

6 *and raised us up together and made us sit together in the heavenly places in Christ Jesus.*

God made us to sit like kings on the throne with Jesus.

ROMANS 5:17; 8:17

5:17 *For if by the one man's offense death reigned through the one, much more those who receive abundance of grace and of the gift of righteousness will reign in life through the One, Jesus Christ.*

8:17 *and if children, then heirs – heirs of God and joint heirs with Christ, if indeed we suffer with Him, that we may also be glorified together.*

How then do we dare to have a poverty mentality? We must go back to the beginning, make a new start and bring our thoughts into line with the thoughts of God. He wants to bless us, but we have to put ourselves into agreement with Him. Confessions are a good way for us to change our thinking. Go through the Word of God and find Scriptures that speak of financial prosperity and make confessions out of these verses. In the meantime, here are some confessions with which to begin:

I am made in the image of God.
(Gen 1:26)
I have dominion on this earth through Jesus Christ my Lord.
(Luke 10:19)
God has destined me to possess wealth.
(2 Cor 9:8)
I am a son or daughter of God.
(Rom 8:17)
God has given me all things.
(2 Pet 1:3)
God makes me rich.
(2 Cor 8:9)
I bear much fruit.
(John 15:1-8)
Because I am His child, God blesses me abundantly.
(Rom 8:16,17)
Everything I do prospers.
(Ps 1:3)

CHAPTER TWO

MONEY BELONGS TO GOD

Concerning money there are several Biblical principles that
we need to know – principles which reveal the attitudes of
God and His intentions towards His people on the earth. The
first principle that needs to be established is that the wealth of
the earth belongs to God.

PRINCIPLE NUMBER ONE:
WEALTH BELONGS TO GOD!

Let's begin by defining wealth. Wealth is the possession,
in one way or another, of a material which is considered by
others to be precious and having value, such as land, silver or
gold, oil, mineral rights, stocks, and of course cash. All these
riches belong to God.

You might say: "Yes, but I work for a living and I earn my
money." Wake up and hear the news: money belongs to God.
In the Garden of Eden God instructed man to work.

GENESIS 2:15
Then the Lord God took the man and put him in the Garden of Eden to tend and keep it.

Working is part of life on this earth. The minute we realize that all the money in the world – and that includes yours and mine – belongs to God, we are on the road to victory in prosperity.

PSALM 50:10, 12
10 *For every beast of the forest is Mine, and the cattle on a thousand hills.*
12 *If I were hungry, I would not tell you; for the world is Mine and all its fullness.*

HAGGAI 2:8
The silver is Mine, and the gold is Mine, says the Lord of hosts.

That leaves nothing for us to possess, not for you and not for me. All belongs to God.

Someone told me that only 10 percent of the gold deposits in the earth have been claimed and are currently being mined. Maybe the Lord is saving the remaining 90 percent for Christians who have the faith to dig a shaft. It is very costly to dig a gold mine, but the man or woman who submits themselves to the ways of the Holy Spirit will find a less costly way to mine gold.

Oil is another valuable resource. Several years ago a group of Christian oil prospectors from Texas decided that there must be oil in Israel. They had read in the Bible that when the Promised Land was divided among the tribes of Israel, the tribe of Asher was given the land where one could find oil.

Using different passages of the Bible, these prospectors gathered information in order to determine the exact location where the oil could be found. They received the authorization from the Israeli government to drill a well and pump the oil, however, they did not find any. Oil has a tendency to move around underground, so maybe today it can be found just a little farther east in the hands of the Arabs! God keeps a calendar concerning these things. I believe that at the end of the time of the Gentiles, Israel will be able to pump all the oil she wants!

The wealth of the world is at the disposal of the Lord to do with as He pleases and in the period of time that He chooses. But it is true, also, that we have a role to play in order to obtain riches. Our role is to listen to the Holy Spirit and to obey the voice of the Lord; otherwise we will be digging wells of oil that the Lord has not called us to dig. God is always ready to prosper us, but we must let Him determine the manner in which He chooses to give us prosperity. We must be led by the Holy Spirit.

The second principle to establish is that God wants His people to have the wealth of the world.

THE SECOND PRINCIPLE:
GOD WANTS US TO HAVE THE WEALTH!

3 JOHN 2
Beloved, I pray that you may prosper in all things and be in health, just as your soul prospers.

Notice how the Word of God says, **"prosper in all things"**. That means the things of this world, the things that one can touch, taste and see. Do you realize that Proverbs 13:22 says that the wealth of the sinner is saved up for the righteous? It is not God's will that the unsaved people have all the wealth of the world. In the Old Testament our prosperity was a part of the covenant that God made with Abraham.

DEUTERONOMY 8:18
And you shall remember the Lord your God, for it is He who gives you power to get wealth, that He may establish His covenant which He swore to your fathers, as it is this day.

We can see that God had given us the power to get wealth when we read the following passage:

GALATIANS 3:6, 7
6 just as Abraham "believed God and it was accounted to him for righteousness".
7 Therefore know that only those who are of faith are sons of Abraham.

GALATIANS 3:13, 14
13 Christ has redeemed us from the curse of the law having become a curse for us (for it is written, "Cursed is everyone who hangs on a tree"),
14 that the blessing of Abraham might come upon the Gentiles in Christ Jesus, that we might receive the promise of the Spirit through faith.

Now, we are sons of Abraham. Then, if we are sons of Abraham God must give us the power to get wealth because God made a covenant with Abraham which we read in Genesis 12:2, 3 and also in:

GENESIS 15:1
After these things the word of the Lord came to Abram in a vision, saying, Do not be afraid, Abram, I am your shield, your exceedingly great reward.

GALATIANS 3:29
And if you are Christ's, then you are Abraham's seed, and heirs according to the promise.

That means that you and I already have the power to get wealth; it only remains for us to bring it into manifestation in our lives through our faith. Once we realize that the promise is for us – that the covenant for wealth is for us – we simply believe it and receive it. Just like the Scriptures say:

MARK 11:24
Therefore I say to you, whatever things you ask when you pray, believe that you receive them, and you will have them.

That does not mean you only believe when you pray or for ten minutes after having prayed. It means that you never stop believing. That's why it is really stupid to grab someone and say, "Quick! Agree with me in prayer!" Then you pray and the person says "Amen!" But the next day neither of you can really remember to what you put yourselves into agreement. This sort of prayer is so superficial that it nearly has no value.

HEBREWS 10:35, 36
Therefore do not cast away your confidence, which has great reward. For you have need of endurance, so that after you have done the will of God, you may receive the promise:

First of all, we are to believe that it is truly the will of God for us to be wealthy; believe that His will is to bring us to the place of obtaining wealth; then, continue to believe with confidence. While we are waiting to receive, stay in an attitude of joy and gratitude. Have a steady expectation that the Holy Spirit is guiding us towards these riches.

The third principle that we must establish is that God does not want the wealth of the world <u>to have us and to dominate us.</u>

THE THIRD PRINCIPLE:
MONEY MUST NOT HAVE US!

1 TIMOTHY 6:10
For the love of money is a root of all kinds of evil, for which some have strayed from the faith in their greediness, and pierced themselves through with many sorrows.

Do you realize that the people who say that money is the root of all evil believe that the Bible says that? But what the Bible says, in fact, is that the <u>love</u> of money is the root of all evil. Since we have the power to get wealth, we must become "clean". God cannot make us prosperous if we have evil motivations such as greed or selfishness, which are the love of money.

JAMES 4:3
You ask and do not receive because you ask amiss that you may spend it on your pleasures.

Years ago we bought a portion of a business that owned and operated four restaurants. In order to do that we had to sell a building that we owned. We lived in that building which included two other flats. We needed the money not only to buy into the restaurants, but also to buy a house for us. We sold this building to a real estate investor who knew all the ins and outs of real estate laws. He persuaded us to give the title to him right away and he would pay us in three large payments. We accepted. It seemed right and our lawyers told us it was a good deal.

The investor gave us the first payment. Then he sold the building to a bank. He contracted for the bank to pay us the next two payments but in this transaction we lost $50,000. We felt that the $50,000 rightfully belonged to us so we took out a lawsuit against the man and the bank. One of the two owed us the money!

The real estate investor took his money that he had received from the bank and left the country. So we continued our lawsuit against the bank and we lost! Not only that but two weeks later, the bank took out a lawsuit against us demanding $100,000! We were a bit disconcerted to say the least! I ran to the Lord. "Lord! I thought you were in this with us! How could it have gone so wrong?" He asked me a question in return, **"What was your motivation?"**

I had to go back and search my heart. My motivation was greed. I thought that money was mine and greed ran rampant in my heart. I prostrated myself before the Lord and asked Him to wash me and cleanse me from this greed and this attraction toward money. Then we went to the bank and told them that we had been wrong. What would it cost us to satisfy them? They said if we would pay them $17,000 they would drop the lawsuit. So we paid them. But the Lord is so full of grace! When we get ourselves clean, He makes up the loss. One month later we received a check, totally unexpected, for the exact sum of $17,000. Since then God has given us many times over the $50,000 we lost in the building.

Never forget: the wealth of the world belongs to the Lord. Money belongs to God. God wants us to have wealth. He gives us the power to get wealth. But he does not want the wealth of the world to have us. Money is not the root of all evil. The love of money is the root of all evil.

CHAPTER THREE

THE ABUNDANT LIFE

People try to hang onto money as if it belonged to them. Someone told me about a system for catching monkeys. The hunter puts a little piece of food in a container with a small opening into which a monkey can only slide its hand. Once the monkey takes hold of the food it is impossible for him to pull his fist out again. One would think the monkey would drop the food the minute he sees the hunter approaching. But no, even when the hunter puts the sack over its head to bring it into captivity, the monkey does not let go of the food. That's the same kind of behavior human beings demonstrate with money.

However, that is not the system or the way of God. His system is that His people learn how to give – how to let go of money – how to release it to Him who in His turn will multiply it back to us.

LUKE 6:38
Give, and it will be given to you, good measure, pressed

down, shaken together, and running over will be put into your bosom. For with the same measure that you use, it will be measured back to you.

The fourth principle to establish is the tithe.

THE FOURTH PRINCIPLE:
THE TITHE BELONGS TO GOD!

To give God ten percent of all you have goes back to the time of Abraham. Then Moses put it into writing for us.

LEVITICUS 27:30
And all the tithe of the land, whether of the seed of the land or of the fruit of the tree, is the Lord's. It is holy to the Lord.

Some people say, "But that was for the Israelites. We don't have to give the tithe. We've been redeemed from the curse of the law." I've got news for you. Abraham lived before the law. The tithe is always in place. God requires it in the New Covenant.

HEBREWS 7:8
Here mortal men receive tithes, but there he receives them, of whom it is witnessed that he lives.

When we pay our tithes we do indeed give them to mortal men, but in reality we give them to Jesus. Each penny given to the Church, to those in need, or to other works of God must be consecrated to Jesus. In fact the tithe means to give ten percent to Jesus. We can often have problems giving our tithe to mortal men because we don't entirely trust them to use the money with wisdom. But in reality we give our tithes to Jesus. Then what the men do with the money concerns only the Lord. God registers our tithes in heaven and in that way we don't have to concern ourselves with what becomes of the money.

Since God is the owner of our money, whether we want it that way or not, not giving Him His ten percent makes the ninety percent becomes "infected" and those who don't give can't prosper. It's as if the money was stolen from our account. The majority of the people who hold back the ten percent do so out of fear.

1 PETER 5:6, 7
Therefore humble yourselves under the mighty hand of God, that He may exalt you in due time, casting all your care upon Him, for He cares for you.

We humble ourselves by acting according to the ways of God. We unburden ourselves by giving our worries to Him. Let Him occupy Himself with the payment of our bills. When we have humbled ourselves under the powerful hand of God in giving Him His ten percent, we are in His perfect will. Then He is free to take care of us. But when we don't give Him His ten percent we are out of His perfect will. Satan then has the right to devour our ninety percent!

Before my husband and I started giving our tithe, we earned a good income. But we never seemed to have anything. We couldn't go out to eat; we couldn't go on vacation. It was impossible for us to do well with our money. We lived as poor people while earning a lot. Then we began paying our tithe. What happened was extraordinary because we didn't earn any more than before, but the ninety percent went farther and lasted longer. Satan was no longer devouring our money.

Before leaving the United States to move to France, we received a large amount of money and I put it in the bank. I didn't have any intention of keeping the tithe, but for one reason or another I just didn't give it. I think it was really a matter of laziness. Then the problems began. Our oven exploded. That cost $400 to repair! The electric pump on our swimming pool blew up and that cost $800 to buy a new one, actually a rebuilt one that carried no guarantees. Then the swimming pool mysteriously emptied itself overnight. That meant the new pump was ruined.

Suddenly the light dawned. Run to God and ask Him what was going on! God never changes. From Him come only blessings. If so many negative things were happening then it must be me who needed to change. I must have done something to get out from underneath His protective hand. The Lord answered my question quite simply, **"Where's My tithe?"** Believe me I put a check in the mail that same day!

When the repairman came for the second time to look at the swimming pool pump, just after I had paid the tithe, he said, "Your pump has had a miracle! It did burn up, I can see the marks, but it works perfectly."

The fifth principle (and it is here that most Christians miss it) is understanding the difference between tithes and offerings.

THE FIFTH PRINCIPLE:
OFFERINGS ARE BEYOND THE TITHE!

The tithe and offerings are two entirely different things. The tithe is the first ten percent of our revenue. Offerings are beyond that and are more than the tithe.

MALACHI 3:8,10
8 Will a man rob God? Yet you have robbed Me! But you say, In what way have we robbed You? In tithes and offerings.
10 Bring all the tithes into the storehouse that there may be food in My house, and try Me now in this, says the Lord of hosts, if I will not open for you the windows of heaven and pour out for you such blessing that there will not be room enough to receive it.

These verses speak of the tithe, but the following speak of offerings.

LUKE 6:38
Give, and it will be given to you, good measure, pressed down, shaken together, and running over will be put into your bosom. For with the same measure that you use, it will be measured back to you.

This verse is not concerned with the tithe because tithes are not something that we can give. The tithe does not belong to us. We return the tithes to God because they belong to Him in the first place.

PROVERBS 3:9
Honor the Lord with your possessions, and with the firstfruits of all your increase;

Your possessions are the ninety percent that God puts at your disposal. A certain couple has written a book detailing how they give ninety percent of their income to God. They started by giving one or two percent beyond their tithe. Then they did more and more. The more they gave, the more God returned to them. God will move heaven and earth to put money in the hands of people willing to invest it in His work.

This couple did not deprive themselves of any of the pleasures that money can bring. They own boats, planes, fur coats and big houses. They live in abundance. But ninety percent of their income goes to building hospitals, orphanages and churches around the world. They support missionaries. Their money works for God. This man started as a simple carpenter but now he owns an international construction business. Like this couple, when we work for God, He works for us.

LEVITICUS 2:12
As for the offering of the firstfruits, you shall offer them to the Lord....

Another type of offering is that of firstfruits. This is not the tithe; this is designed to secure the harvest from which you will tithe. When the first of something comes to you, you take the best of whatever it is and offer it to the Lord. Another verse calls it a sheaf which clearly is not everything that comes in early, but a portion. Another verse calls it your best gift, meaning you determine what it is you can stretch yourself to give, however you still go to the Lord to find out where He wants the gift to go.

Firstfruits seems to me like an insurance policy. You take the very first thing you receive, that which could benefit you, and instead of using it yourself you sacrifice, give it to the Lord and He, in turn, multiples your continuing harvest. For instance, as a writer, when I have completed a book I take the first volumes I receive from the publisher and I give them away. Having waited so long to receive the finished product I am eager for sales, but I send them out as a gift from the Lord, since it is His book anyway! And yes, I send them to the ones He tells me to send them to.

The Holy Spirit knows where our offerings should go.

1 CORINTIIIANS 2:11
For what man knows the things of a man except the spirit of the man which is in him? Even so no one knows the things of God except the Spirit of God

We all know good people and good causes that need money. But unless the Lord reveals it, no one can see into the spirit of a man or into the motivations of a ministry. Therefore, it works best to wait for the Holy Spirit to tell us where to give. Our money is like a seed, and we want to plant our seed in good soil – His ground – because the earth of God is good ground.

PHILIPPIANS 4:6
Be anxious for nothing, but in everything by prayer and supplication, with thanksgiving, let your requests be made known to God.

Good people and good works must present their requests to God and God will watch over the provision of their financial needs. When God knows that you are waiting for Him to provide your needs, He will do everything in His power to bring the money to you that you need. That is not to say that a Pastor cannot receive offerings for different projects. No. It is very important that a Pastor receive offerings and tithes from the congregation. In this manner he is giving his people the opportunity to be blessed because we are blessed in giving our tithes and offerings.

The Lord chose a marvelous way to teach me about offerings so that I would truly understand them. I have an aunt that I love very much who lived about two hours away by car in the foothills of California. She is the one who led me to the Lord so she will always hold a special place in my heart. As I was driving to her house for a weekend the Lord said to me, **"There is a man in this city who wants to start a Cassette Ministry. I want you to give him all the equipment he needs to get started."**

I said, "If this is really You speaking to me Lord, then I am not going to say a word to anyone. You must show me this man." When I arrived I did not mention it to my aunt; I didn't even know if she knew anybody like that.

On Sunday we attended her Church. As I opened the door to go inside I saw a man coming out of a door across the foyer. He came directly to me with his hand outstretched ready to shake mine and said, "Welcome to our Church."

The words that came out of my mouth shocked me. "Are you the man who wants to start a Cassette Ministry?"

An observer would have thought I hit him. He staggered back, almost falling, and said, "Yes!"

I said, "The Lord told me to give you the recording equipment you need." I took his name and address and promised to bring the materials to him.

I found a ministry called "Firefighters for Christ" who sold recording equipment to Christian ministries at wholesale prices. I was able to buy duplicators, blank cassettes, labels and everything this man could need for his ministry. Putting it all in the trunk of my car I drove the two hours up to his address. When I pulled up to the door I was horrified! The building was so old the sight of it was appalling. It was a wreck! I said, "Lord! Are you sure you want this shiny new equipment given to whatever is inside that ruined building? Have I made a huge mistake?"

But I went inside with the equipment and asked the man who met me at the door, "Who are you? I don't know anything about you!" He showed me around the building. It was a Christian Coffee Bar and youth from the whole area gathered there. This man had been a professional golfer but with the leading of the Lord he quit his career and started the Coffee Bar. The city in which the Coffee Bar was located happened to be the center of drug activity for the region. But the leader of the drug traffic had visited the Coffee Bar and this ex golf pro had led him to the Lord. He enrolled in Bible School and the drug ring no longer exists!

The ex golf pro showed me a brochure he had made which stated he had a Cassette Ministry. He said, "I wrote that by faith." I learned that day what the Bible means when it says, **"It is more blessed to give than to receive."**

To evangelize the world costs money.

1 CORINTHIANS 9:7
Whoever goes to war at his own expense? Who plants a vineyard and does not eat of its fruit? Or who tends a flock and does not drink of the milk of the flock?

We Christians have an enemy, Satan. He violently opposes the spreading of the Gospel of our Lord Jesus Christ. In order to overcome him we must have money. We need money to run the local Church, to send Missionaries, to produce Christian radio programs, to print books and produce Christian television. All these things cost money. All the great work of God needs money in order to operate. This is the hour for the Church. It's time the financial barriers came down! The key to abundance is to support the evangelization of the world. If God can get the money <u>through you</u>, He will get it <u>to you.</u>

People constantly give me good reasons to explain the wealth of the United States. They say that comes from never having had a world war on our land. We have so many natural resources. The United States has an aggressive spirit, etc.... All that is true, but I have a question to ask. If those are the reasons, then why isn't Mexico rich? All those reasons apply to them as well.

There is only one explanation for why the United States is a rich nation. The Christians of our country have learned the principle of giving. The United States has sent and is still sending ninety percent of the missionaries to the world. God honors and blesses a nation that does His work.

God wants to honor and bless the United States even more. Money belongs to God. He wants us to have it, but He does not want money to have us. God commands us to give Him our tithe and if we do it, in return He will multiply our money. Our tithes and offerings finance His work on the earth: the tithe pays for the Church and the offerings pay for the evangelization of the world.

Satan wants to bring doubt to our thought life regarding financial prosperity, but we must respond to him with the Word of God:

Christ became poor so that I could become rich.
(2 Corinthians 8:9)
God gives me the power to get wealth.
(Deuteronomy 8:18)
God takes care of me.
(1 Peter 5:7)
I am blessed in all that I undertake.
(Psalm 1:3)
After I have repented, even my mistakes prosper! The Lord
fills my storehouses.
(Deuteronomy 28:8)!

I deposit my money in my wallet, in my stocks, in my bank accounts and in my investments. God fills my storehouses! God blesses me in all things.

CHAPTER FOUR

PRACTICING "SEED FAITH GIVING"

Seed Faith Giving has a bad reputation and I think that comes from the fact that those who teach it don't understand Seed Faith Giving. I heard of a Frenchman who traveled around his country telling audiences to give him a certain amount of money. He told them that in doing so they would harvest a great amount of money in return. He received large sums and moved to Florida! Even though he made out like a bandit, that's not how Seed Faith works. Just because people abuse the principle does not mean that Seed Faith Giving is wrong. It is, in fact, a Biblical principle.

MARK 4:26-29
26 And He said, The kingdom of God is as if a man should scatter seed on the ground,
27 and should sleep by night and rise by day, and the seed should sprout and grow, he himself does not know how.
28 For the earth yields crops by itself; first the blade, then the head, after that the full grain in the head.

29 But when the grain ripens, immediately he puts in the sickle, because the harvest has come.

A seed of money planted in the kingdom of God produces a harvest for the person who planted the seed. A dear friend of mine was in the throes of divorce. Her husband left her for a younger woman. My friend threw herself into the arms of the Lord and sought His advice with more fervor than ever before. Even though he was very rich, her future former husband didn't want to give her a cent. Her lawyer expressed his concern that she would lose everything and advised her not to spend a single dime she didn't have to spend. She only owned a few stocks in a company, but they had never paid her any interest. After having been married for 36 years and raising children, my friend found herself having to find work and that did not excite her at all. She consulted the Lord and He said, **"Plant a seed".**

Soon after, to her surprise, the stocks she owned rendered her a payout for $10,000. She received the check by mail. Opening the envelope on her way out the door for a special meeting at Church, she put the check in her purse. The speaker that night asked for a special offering to be taken to raise funds for the construction of the Church building. My friend could hear the Lord saying, **"Plant a seed. Plant a seed."** But she could also hear her lawyer saying, "Save every dime. Save every dime."

To her dismay the Evangelist said, "There is a woman here who could give $10,000 if she wanted!"

Right away she said, "Alright, Lord, I'll plant a seed, but no one must know about it."

Then the Evangelist said, "Will that woman please stand up?" Unwillingly, my friend stood. Seated in the back row she hoped no one would recognize her and run tell her lawyer, or her children or her future former husband. Naturally the Evangelist then asked, "Will you please come forward so we can pray for you?" My friend would have rather slid under the pew, but she obeyed and went forward for prayer.

The next day her Pastor called and told her he was returning her check because her face looked so dismal when she came forward for prayer. However, she insisted that he keep it. He asked if she understood Seed Faith Giving and she said no. He explained that when a farmer plants a seed he doesn't know how it is going to produce a harvest because the seed accomplishes that all by itself. We act in the same way with our gifts to God. We give, we expect God to multiply our gift without knowing how He will do it and He does it faithfully.

My friend stopped worrying and started trusting God for the harvest. In six months those same stocks brought her 400 times her seed! She never had to find a job.

ISAIAH 55:10-11
10 For as the rain comes down and the snow from heaven and do not return there but water the earth and make it bring forth and bud that it may give seed to the sower and bread to the eater.
11 So shall My word be that goes forth from My mouth; it shall not return to Me void, but it shall accomplish what I please and it shall prosper in the thing for which I sent it.

This passage fills me with joy! The Word of God waters, fertilizes and makes to grow what the Word of God says! His Word says that Christ became poor so that we could become rich (2 Corinthians 8:9). When we let this Word water us and we are filled to the full with it, the Word will grow and produce fruit.

The Word of God says He furnishes seed to the sower and bread to the eater. It does not depend on our ingenuity, our ability or our intelligence, but it is the Word of God that produces that which we need. His Word accomplishes His will and brings His plans to pass. We must learn to use His Word.

2 CORINTHIANS 9:6-10
6 But this I say: He who sows sparingly will also reap sparingly, and he who sows bountifully will also reap bountifully.
7 So let each one give as he purposes in his heart, not grudgingly or of necessity; for God loves a cheerful giver.
8 And God is able to make all grace abound toward you, that you, always having all sufficiency in all things, may have an abundance for every good work.
9 As it is written: He has dispersed abroad. He has given to the poor; His righteousness endures forever.
10 Now may He who supplies seed to the sower, and bread for food, supply and multiply the seed you have sown and increase the fruits of your righteousness.

In this passage the seed is compared to money. Chapters 8 and 9 of 2 Corinthians talk only about money. But in the passage from Isaiah that Paul quotes, the seed is compared to the Word of God. The message of these two passages is that the seed of money planted in the Kingdom of God – the spreading of the Word of God – produces a harvest for the person who planted the seed.

When I began to learn this principle I didn't understand what constituted a "seed". Was a seed my tithe or my offering? The Lord answered my question by saying, **"A seed is a seed."** That is to say that a seed is both tithe and offering. Each time that I pay my tithe or give my offerings, I make specific requests for the provision of my needs and the accomplishment of my desires. And I see fruit from my seeds.

A friend of mine wanted a Harley Davidson motorcycle. At the bottom of each check he wrote for his tithe or his offering, he marked, "This is for my Harley Davidson." After several months of doing this, with his wife laughing at him the whole time, someone gave him a brand new Harley Davidson! Now his wife is writing on the bottom of her tithe and offering checks, "This is for my new furniture."

After all, when a farmer plants seeds he doesn't say, "I have no idea what is going to grow there." No, after having planted sunflower seeds sunflowers will grow in that field and soybeans will grow where soybean seeds have been planted, also cotton, etc. When we plant seeds we can also expect a certain harvest, a harvest that we determine before planting.

Some people might say, "You're trying to buy God!" No, not at all. I am using God's system. Look again at what His Word says.

2 CORINTHIANS 9:6-8
6 But this I say; He who sows sparingly will also reap sparingly,

and he who sows bountifully will also reap bountifully.
7 So let each one give as he purposes in his heart, not grudgingly or of necessity; for God loves a cheerful giver.
8 And God is able to make all grace abound toward you, that you, always having all sufficiency in all things, may have an abundance for every good work.

Our abundance depends on our joyous generosity. When we give to the Lord with joy – a sincere and pure joy – He fills us with all good things so that not only do we possess all that we need but we also have an abundance for sharing. If a farmer sowed seeds with this attitude: "Oh this stuff doesn't work. I won't get a harvest out of this." If he never waters his seed, doesn't check his field and hasn't any faith in his harvest, he won't receive anything. When a seed is planted it must be watered and cultivated. A farmer must believe that he is going to have a harvest; otherwise he won't watch over his field.

One time in the back of my property I planted some corn. I'd never planted corn before. Likewise my neighbor planted corn and when our stalks were knee high he came over and said, "Oh, no! You've done it all wrong. You'll never get any ears of corn from those stalks." His criticism totally discouraged me and I abandoned my corn. In the fall I went to dig up those forgotten stalks and found dozens of dried up ears of corn that I could have enjoyed in the summer if I had not abandoned my crop.

We must not abandon our Seed Faith Giving crop! Paul speaks of this process.

1 CORINTHIANS 3:6
I planted, Apollos watered, but God gave the increase.

Paul and Apollos carried the Word of God to the Corinthians and God made them to prosper and grow in His Word. In the same way, after having planted my seed in the Word of God, I water it with more Word. I give, then each day I repeat the Scriptures that promise prosperity. I pray for the people or the places that have received my seed, such as my Church, a missionary or another work in the Kingdom of God. I thank God daily for my harvest and I sincerely expect to receive my crop from my Father.

Some seeds take more time than others to grow. Why? I don't know. But I have learned one thing. If I stop believing that I am going to receive, the harvest will be ruined. The Bible explains this destruction.

HEBREWS 10:35-36
35 *Therefore do not cast away your confidence, which has great reward.*
36 *For you have need of endurance, so that after you have done the will of God, you may receive the promise.*

In Tulsa, Oklahoma, there is a wonderful Church that grew so fast that in seven years it had 8,000 members. However, they did not have a building. The Lord told the Pastor to build one without borrowing any money. He needed millions of dollars to build as big a building as he needed but the Lord wanted to demonstrate to this congregation that they could have confidence in Him.

PHILIPPIANS 4:19
And my God shall supply all your need according to His riches in glory by Christ Jesus.

Many Churches are slaves to the system of the world because they are indebted to banks for money to build their buildings. The interest they pay eats up all their money and nothing is left for spreading the Word of God in the world or for helping other people. Mortgages are a trap of the devil for the Churches. In my first weeks of attending Bible School, this Church organized a special campaign to raise the money for the building project. The Lord told the Pastor if each one would make a promise of $1,000, He would accomplish His Word and supply the seed for the sower and each one would receive a harvest. Many answered this call to consecrate $1,000 to the Lord. The Pastor asked them to come forward.

At this point my husband and I had $8,000, period. We had closed our bank accounts in California and all our money was in traveler's checks. We did have 50% interest in four restaurants in California but we didn't receive any money from that partnership, having left them in the hands of our partner to sell. They had already been on the market for one year without anyone showing any interest. We didn't know when we would receive more money. This $8,000 had to pay for our Bible School, our son's tuition and upkeep in the University of California, our rent, the airplane to California for my husband and our son and all our expenses during what would probably be a long time.

Therefore we decided to be brave in our faith. We went forward and not only consecrated our money, but actually gave $1,000 to the Lord, signing the traveler's checks that night. One month later, we received a check for $40,000 from an unexpected source (yet another wonderful story)! During this same meeting where we gave $1,000, some new acquaintances of ours also went forward to consecrate their money. However, they did not have full confidence in the Word of God.

They didn't stand on the Bible verses that promise prosperity and they didn't pray for the building fund or for the Church. Instead they began to complain. They thought that the Pastor had deceived them and embarrassed them. In a fit of anger they changed Churches. Soon after they were living in poverty and could barely pay for their food.

The Word of God is true!

NUMBERS 23:19
God is not a man that He should lie.

His Word says,

LUKE 6:38
Give and it will be given unto you.

The Church in Tulsa was built in three years without incurring any debt. The seed of faith works. A seed of money, sown in the Kingdom of God, produces a harvest for the person who plants with faith.

Sometimes the harvest is slow to produce. Once I had to wait five years to receive something that I wanted, each day thanking the Lord by faith for that which I had received from Him. For five years! Some people give up and accept defeat, but God said that His Word would not come back to Him without accomplishing His will. Therefore I feed myself continually on His Word in order to grow and I act as if His Word is true, even though I don't as yet have anything to show for my faith.

Essentially, that is faith: to believe in Jesus and in His Word, even if we don't see Him, even if we don't see the result of what He said.

HEBREWS 11:1
Now faith is the substance of things hoped for, the evidence of things not seen.

One time I asked the Lord, "Why is this answer taking so long?"

He said, "The money will be there when you need it." He led me to this Scripture.

HABAKKUK 2:2-3
2 Then the Lord answered me and said: Write the vision and make it plain on tablets, that he may run who reads it.
3 For the vision is yet for an appointed time; but at the end it will speak, and it will not lie. Though it tarries, wait for it; because it will surely come, it will not tarry.

I like to keep track of the harvests I am expecting. I take the Bible at its Word. There are moments, however, when panic will set in and I speak words that annul my belief. Words like, "All is lost!" "I'm going to be poor forever!" "If I don't receive my harvest pretty soon I'm going to be ruined!"

As quickly as I can regroup myself I ask God to forgive me and cleanse me of this unrighteousness as I know that without faith I cannot be pleasing to God. Then I take the paper where I have written the vision, or rather the harvests I am expecting, and I put myself once again in faith to receive.

Personally, I don't believe in debt. It is not good to spend money one does not have. People who fill out "faith checks", believing that the Lord will stock up their accounts before the check is cashed, are deluding themselves and breaking the law. Here's how I see it: we must believe the money will be there and actually, in reality, receive it before spending it. I don't believe having debt is a bad thing. I just believe that not having debt is better.

DEUTERONOMY 15:6
For the Lord your God will bless you just as He promised you; you shall lend to many nations, but you shall not borrow; you shall reign over many nations, but they shall not reign over you.

To be a slave to money is exhausting. It is wise to content ourselves with what we have at the same time as expecting to receive more from God. This helps us to stay out of debt. It is also wise to keep our priorities in order: the first tenth of our revenue belongs to the Lord. Then we can take care of our family.

1 TIMOTHY 5:8
But if anyone does not provide for his own, and especially for those of his household, he has denied the faith and is worse than an unbeliever.

I've heard of people who have committed rash acts with Seed Faith Giving. For example, they have given their entire paycheck to God and that leaves them with nothing for the rest of the month. That's nonsense! The Holy Spirit leads us to give the right amount and He shows us to whom it should be given. Don't try to be more intelligent than God! Learn to obey Him only and to follow Him. Always remember, it is love that makes this financial blessing work in our lives.

1 CORINTHIANS 13:3
And though I bestow all my goods to feed the poor, and though I give my body to be burned, but have not love, it profits me nothing.

If the love of God does not flow from our hearts, we will not prosper. We can give all the money we want, but if greed or selfishness is our motivation, we will receive nothing from the Lord. We must love the people of the country to which we send a missionary. We must love the people who occupy the building that we are helping to build.

In Tulsa I met a man who told me he had planted a seed in each good ministry in that city without having ever received a harvest of any kind. The bank foreclosed on his house and he had a hard time feeding his family. In speaking with him I discovered that his only motivation in giving to God was to become rich. One does not mock God. We must judge ourselves so that we will not be judged.

We have been created in the image of God and we have dominion on the earth. God has provided wealth for us because we are His children. In Christ He has given us all things. He has made us rich and prospered us and in Him we increase abundantly.

The wealth belongs to God, but He gives it to us. God requires that we give Him the tithe and then He blesses us. He asks that we give offerings beyond our tithe and He multiplies that money back to us. Our tithes and offerings serve to accomplish His work on the earth: the tithe for the Church and the offerings for the evangelization of the world. That is the system of God.

LUKE 6:38
Give and it will be given to you, good measure, pressed down, shaken together and running over will be put into your bosom. For with the same measure that you use, it will be measured back to you.

THE END OF MY BOOK

THE BEGINNING OF YOUR WEALTH

YOUR MISSIONARY, MARTY DELMON

For me it all started when I spent months in a deep depression contemplating suicide until someone invited me to a prayer meeting in the northern hills of California on a hot summer night. Having no air conditioning, the Pastor pulled chairs into the parking lot and put them in a circle. When seated, there were twelve of us.

As we closed our eyes it occurred to me I had never really prayed. Oh sure, I threw prayers to heaven in desperate times, but I never waited for an answer. Now I was willing to try it. When I closed my eyes I saw a bright white light in the middle of the circle that emitted such heat I thought my skin would peel off. A wind came from that ball of light that pushed my hair back from my head.

My logical mind said the sun was setting and hitting me full on and that a strong wind had come up. I opened one eye to see the sun had already set and there wasn't even a breeze in the trees. I closed my eye again. The phenomenon remained. Not to be rude by opening my eyes, or getting up to leave, I sat and watched. Suddenly Jesus stepped out of the light, held out his arms and said, "Come unto Me."

I started to get out of my chair and go to Him when the Pastor said "Amen." Obliged to open my eyes, the apparition disappeared. What I thought took two minutes, actually occurred over two hours. I had been entranced with Jesus for two hours! When I left that prayer meeting, Jesus went with me. He talked to me every day. I started going to church. I felt better and better about myself.

One day while walking to church I heard an audible voice. It said, **"Marty, you've come a long way but you have one more step to take."** So shocked to hear an audible voice, I simply asked, *"What?"*

The voice responded, "You must say with your mouth that I am your Lord." I knew it was Jesus speaking, nonetheless, rage rose up in me. No one would be my Lord, but me! However, I instinctively knew that if I refused I would lose His companionship and I didn't want that because He made me feel good about myself.

The church I attended had an altar rail where we knelt to take communion. I wrestled with my decision all through the service, so when I knelt at that rail I looked up at the cross and said, "Jesus, You are my Lord." Something cold and awful left my body through my feet and something warm and wonderful flooded me from the front, filling me with love and peace and joy. Since that day I have belonged to Jesus and my life has never been the same.

I consider it a privilege to serve in the Army of Jesus Christ as His Ambassador. My job is to go into all the world preaching the Gospel and teaching people His Lordship. He has commissioned me for this: I'm a story teller. The Lord told me that "The Spirit of the Lord God is upon Me, because the Lord has anointed me to preach good tidings to the poor through stories. He has sent me to heal the brokenhearted through stories. To proclaim liberty to the captives through stories."

Here's what I do: Wherever I am, I take people's testimonies. If their story is a complete one, a beginning, a middle and an end, I write it as a True Life Testimony. If their story is a vignette, usually just an ending, then I add the beginning and the middle and put it in my series called Stories from My Heart. My third group is called On the Footprints of Jesus. These stories are placed in Biblical times. My current series is entitled Stories of Life.

I started writing stories fifteen years ago. My husband and I came off the mission field, after being there since 1988, because of his homosexual activities. I've written a novel about that called *Sleeping with Demons*. We moved to Sarasota, Florida where I pioneered a church. Though having the time of my life, I answered an altar call for ministers who felt like square pegs in round holes. I expected God to order me back to France but He didn't. He simply said, "Write!" And instantly I knew to write stories and put them on the radio. I didn't even listen to radio! But I knew I had heard from God, so I obeyed.

A Christian station agreed to air them; they opened their studios to me and taught me everything about the medium of radio. However, the day came when I could no longer pay for radio time so I called the station to cancel my contract. The manager said, "That's too bad." The next day he called back. "We had an emergency board meeting last night and you can be on our station for as long as you want, for free. Your stories are reaching the lost and the lost don't know to send in a check to help you pay the radio costs. Only mature Christians know it takes money to spread the Gospel."

Then the Lord told me to tell my stories in person. He gave me the names of three churches for starters. Other churches invited me and my stories spread. In Santa Barbara I accompanied the Pastor's wife while she broadcast her weekly radio program. Thinking to be simply a chauffeur I sat meekly against the back wall. Suddenly they swung an overhead microphone in front of my nose. Alarmed, I asked, "What's this?"

The station manager said, "You're our featured guest this hour." Seeing my look of dismay she asked, "Have you ever done live radio?" I'm sure my eyes were the size of saucers; up until that point I had only done canned radio so I shook my head no. "You'll love it." She said. "We're on in 30 seconds."

I turned to the Pastor's wife. "What do I do?"

"Tell your stories." She replied.

For one hour I told stories. The station manager said, "That was great! Can we air your stories every week? We'll do it for free." Of course I said yes. She looked at me strangely. "You don't know who we are, do you?" I said no and she explained. "We beam our signal to our mother station in Australia and they beam our programs all around the Pacific rim. Your stories will be heard by two thirds of the world."

Only God could have orchestrated that! Our job is to find out what God wants us to do and then do it. He does the rest. But God did call me to the mission field, in fact, to the most difficult mission field in the world: France. Billy Graham calls France the darkest continent, even though it is just a little country. He calls it that because it is such hard ground to plow.

Eleven years ago I returned to France, alone. Some friends in the music industry created a CD with four of my stories in French, putting music and sound effects behind the drama. I sent that demo CD to 16 radio stations, hoping for one or maybe two to accept them -- and all said yes! Today my stories are on 45 stations in seven French speaking countries. I'm working to get more!

France and the French speaking countries are the hardest to reach with the Gospel because they outlawed God over 200 years ago. Today, a Frenchman won't darken the door of a church. Less than 1% are born again. But God is not willing for the French to be lost. There is more Christian blood crying out from the land of France than from any other nation.

Between the years of 1000 and 1200, during the Dark Ages, there was light in France. Someone translated the New Testament into the Languedoc tongue. Making copies by hand and passing them around, people lived what they read and got born again. These rebels from tradition were known as The Perfects, or the Cathars, because they believed, according to the New Testament, that when they were born again their spirits were made perfect. Their new perfect spirits, occupied by the Holy Spirit, then worked on their souls and bodies to bring their whole being into perfection.

The Catholic Church, in its worst moment of history, formed the inquisition to annihilate this movement because the Church did not have revelation about the new birth. An estimated one third of the population of France died by the hands of these emissaries of death.

Another movement came in the 1300s called the Valdois. They picked up where The Perfects left off. This was a more widespread movement spreading into Switzerland, Italy and Spain. The Catholic Church, still in the Dark Ages, labeled them heretics and herded about one third of the population into churches which they burned to the ground. Blood red stones can still be seen at various sites.

Then came the Huguenots, France's version of the Reform spearheaded by Martin Luther. Forty nine percent of the population of France embraced Protestantism. Until Catherine de Medici ordered a slaughter in Paris where some say 80,000 bodies were mounded by the River Seine. Two days later the city of Orleans had its own pile of bodies. The St. Bartholomew Day Massacre swept the country. Forty seven percent of the population of France either fled or were slaughtered.

Can you hear that blood crying out for the redemption of its country? It cries through all the bluster and blunder in these times. God is listening. Listen with Him. Help bring in the harvest.

The Lord told me to seed the clouds with my stories so that He can pour out His Spirit on France in the latter day rain. He has put a thirst in the French hearts and polls show that 20% of the population listens to Christian radio. I polled the stations that air my programs and almost all of them have my stories on every day, several times a day. When I asked how many people listen, the numbers added up to over 12 million. People call in tears wanting to know how they can get Jesus to help them with their lives like He helped the character in the story they heard. The radio staff leads the callers to Christ and helps them find a church.

I'm asking you to send me and be my strong support. We need each other. We're all headed for heaven, but first we must reach the ends of the earth. I'm in France and I'm sending my stories around the world; will you be my supply line for prayer and finances? Will you fulfill your part of the Great Commission by sending me?

There are four ways you can help me. One is to give a big love offering. Two is to sponsor a story. Each story costs $300 to produce. Whoever pays for one story to be translated, recorded, mixed and a master created, your name will be added to the story. The credits will say, "This story was brought to you by – your name, city and state." Every station that receives a copy of that Master will be broadcasting your name as the person or the church or the business who cared enough for the lost to send a story of the Gospel to them.

The third way you can help me is to become my monthly faith partner. It is necessary for me to have a roster of partners who will supply my need while on the field. Please consider sending $30 a month. I don't want anyone to be burdened. If you can send more, that's great.

The fourth way is to come to France on a Prayer Journey. As we visit the most beautiful country in the world, we will stop at key places in the Huguenot history and pray for repentance and restoration of this great move of the Spirit. Please contact Andrea Stine, amorrisstine@gmail.com.

Let me explain faith partnership. Read Philippians 1 starting with verse 3.

V 3: *I thank my God upon every remembrance of you.* – I'm sure Paul had a system for remembering his partners. I remember you by keeping your names in a prayer book and praying over the names every day.

V 4: *Always in every prayer of mine making request for you all with joy.* – Let me ask you a question. What requests was Paul making? When the Lord first asked me that question I couldn't answer it. We'll read the answer a little further along.

V 5: *For your fellowship in the gospel from the first day until now.* -- The word fellowship in Greek means partnership. Paul was writing to his partners.

V 6: *Being confident of this very thing, that He who has begun a good work in you will complete it until the day of Jesus Christ.*

Jesus is the one who starts the partnership and He is the one who finishes it. That's why it's called a faith partnership. He tells you what to give and then He supplies the money for you to give. Let me share with you some real life examples.

A certain man in Canada lived on $15,000 a year. While attending a mission's conference he asked the Lord what He wanted him to give. The Lord told him to become a faith partner and give $25,000 the next year. He almost laughed out loud. He said, "Lord, you know I only live on $15,000. How could I possibly give $25,000?"

The Lord said, "I didn't ask you what you had. I told you what I would supply for you to give next year." The man sheepishly made the faith commitment. A whole year went by with no increase in the man's income. One week before the year ended, he won a Cadillac, which he sold for more than the $25,000. That's how God is. When we obey He gives us more than enough, plenty for us and the amount we pledged.

Turn to Philippians 4 starting with verse 15. From the beginning, with Paul as the first missionary, God has always used the same program. One missionary, many faith partners.

V 15: *Now you Philippians know also that in the beginning of the gospel, when I departed from Macedonia, no church shared with me concerning giving and receiving but you only.* Let me ask you. Who gave? The Philippians. Who received? I always thought it was Paul who received. The Philippians gave their money to Paul who received it. But the Lord corrected me. It was the Philippians who received. Giving and Receiving, Seedtime and Harvest, Planting and Reaping: That's God's principle throughout the Bible. Whoever gives receives from God.

V 16: *For even in Thessalonica you sent aid once and again for my necessities.*

Paul depended on his faith partners to meet his needs. It's no different today. God is sending me and by supporting me, you are fulfilling God's requirements on your life to go into all the world and preach the Gospel.

V 17: *Not that I seek the gift, but I seek the fruit that abounds to your account.*

Remember back in chapter one verse four where Paul was making requests for his partners? This is what he was seeking: fruit to their account. I pray for your fruit. I pray for a 100 fold return for every one who partners with me. I've had people report on windfalls, tax returns, contracts that were worth much more than a100 fold return.

One woman pledged $100 a month. Knowing her poverty I was about to give her card back when the Lord said, "This is not between you and her. This is between me and her." She called me a week later to tell me her brother paid off her credit card debt of $5000. Then a member of her church bought a new car and gave the woman her old car worth $6000. She continues to receive great gifts.

Another woman regularly gives $60 a month. She retired several years ago so I expected her giving to diminish, but it didn't. Every year she tells me she receives more money being retired than she ever made in her career and she can't understand it. I do. It's coming from God.

A young man approached me after a service in England and said the Lord told him to videotape me telling one of my stories. I met him the next day at the river Thames. He showed up with all this beautiful equipment he had bought in faith in obedience to God. I prayed he would receive a 100 fold return for his lovely gift to me.

After the shoot we were having a cup of coffee in a pub when his cell phone rang. It was Creflo Dollar himself asking this young man if he would edit and distribute Creflo's CDs and

DVDs throughout Europe. That was a little more than a 100 fold return!

God is faithful. Obey Him and He will supply. Our goal is to reach the entire French speaking world with the Gospel of Jesus Christ in story form on the radio and then in other languages we'll reach the ends of the earth. A story touches a life and changes it forever.

Asking for donations is a time honored tradition going back to Moses. When God gave Moses the plans for the Tabernacle, He told Moses to go ask the people for money. The people gave until Moses had to tell them to stop. He had enough. Moses built the only Tabernacle in the wilderness. I am the only missionary covering the world with evangelistic stories. In the tradition of Moses I am asking you for money to make these evangelistic radio programs and broadcast them to the lost.

God blesses those who send missionaries. The harvest is His passion. You help me save a soul and God will help you. Jesus is waiting for the harvest before He will return. I am recruiting fellow soldiers to help me pull sinners out of the fire. I need you. God needs you.

To be a part of reaching the world for Jesus Christ, through the broadcast of stories that touch the hearts of the lost and draw them into the Kingdom of God, join me. Become a monthly partner and send a monthly offering to World Missions Ministries, PO Box 12609, Oklahoma City, Oklahoma, 73157. My name is Marty Delmon and my missionary number is 31051.

To sponsor a story with your name, your church's name or your company's name broadcast around the world, send $300 to World Missions Ministries, PO Box 12609, Oklahoma City, Oklahoma, 73157. My name is Marty Delmon and the ministry number to put on the memo line of this check is 31054.

You can order my books by visiting any of these websites:

www.martydelmon.com
www.tatepublishing.com
www.store.rpjandco.com

I'm glad to have you on my team. Pray for me as I pray for you!

MORE BOOKS BY MARTY DELMON

SLEEPING WITH DEMONS
www.tatepublishing.com

Married to a man caught in the trap of sexual deviation, Maggie Dubois takes us on her lone journey through the dark valleys of one-sided marriage. Her passage through the somber alley of longing for love is a story that applies to us all.

Denying the existence of the problem, homosexuality, Maggie is ensnared in the conflict. The climax of the book comes when Maggie breaks through the veil of confusion to recognize the truth and confront the spiritual darkness. Exorcising the evil from her life, Maggie walks free.

"Lessons of Life" could well be a subtitle of this book as Maggie guilelessly shares her insights and revelations of what she discovers as she feels her way through the morass. Her discoveries liberate not only herself but her husband as well. Maggie's victory is everyone's victory: truth and freedom.

BURIED LIES
www.tatepublishing.com

No action evokes as much violent emotion and reaction as does incest. Murder, suicide, hatred, imprisonment, all things ugly in life evolve from this insidious trap set in a female child by her father. Journey with seven women as they confront their past, unearth the lies they have believed about themselves, replacing them with the truth and see the changes made in their lives today. Against all odds, these seven overcame the most heinous of sins: sex forced upon them by Daddy.

Between the ages of eight and 17 my step father perfunctorily raped me. At age 17 I confided in a girl friend and she encouraged me to confront him, asking why he would do such a thing. It never occurred to me I had the personal power to get him to stop, but when I followed her advice, he quit. The trauma stayed with me, however, coloring my future and damaging my potential until I received Jesus as my Lord.

The Holy Spirit led me into a prayer process in which Jesus helped me to uncover the lies I believed about myself because of what happened to me. The important part was that He planted the truth in me to replace those lies. It has made all the difference in my life.

Through the course of interviewing people for the stories I write for radio, I discovered that almost one woman out of two suffered what I suffered in my childhood. I have helped some to unearth the lies and believe the truth, but a book about it will reach far more women than I personally can reach. Therefore I have written *Buried Lies.*

BURIED LIES
COMPANION WORKBOOK

When I came to the Lord I carried a lot of baggage. My illegitimate birth, the continual raping by my stepfather between the ages of 8 and 17, my mother telling me I was too stupid to be a writer so I abandoned my passion, the self-sabotage I committed when I broke up with the love of my life because he was 'too good for me', and then the man I did marry, after ten years of marriage and two children, confessed he was gay.

The Lord gave me a prayer process to clear out the chaos in my life which came not because of all these things that happened to me, but because of the lies I believed about myself because of what happened. I called that book *Buried Lies.* When people read *Buried Lies* they asked me to do a workshop to lead them through the prayer process. I thought this to be good as it took me seven hours to complete my first process simply because the prayer is intensely focused and I wasn't accustomed to praying that thoroughly.

Then they asked for a workbook to take home so that they could continue to pull out lies and plant the truth. I decided to put the whole workshop into the workbook, leaving space at the end for them to go through the process themselves and journal about it.

BURIED LIES COMPANION
WORKBOOK AUDIO BOOK

My publisher came up with the best idea when he put the workbook on CD. He even allowed me to do the recording. Now people can take the workshop anywhere they want and the final of the four CDs leads the listener through the prayer process. There is one more prayer to go through which the Lord also gave me for the purpose of hearing Him more clearly. I call it 'The Garden'.

WILD CARD
www.tatepublishing.com

His dream…. Ron La Fave had charted his path and meticulously pursued it. Deflecting every distraction and breaking his own heart in the process, he persevered to the point of wounding his loved ones as he doggedly attained the success that powered his dreams.

But, Ron failed to recognize the reality of evil. Dreams can be sabotaged from within, yet the threat from without comes like a sidewinder. One strike, one puncture and the aspiration deflates like a party balloon flailing wildly about the room.

Wherever he turned, the serpent hoisted its evil head. His Board of Directors threw him out; his wife left; his mentor disowned him; his bank accounts closed; his reputation tanked and the industry blackballed him. Left with nothing, he retreated to Jackson Hole.

Counting on the mountains to restore him, he hid in the Tetons. However, a certain Presence wouldn't leave. Ron found himself grappling with distractions he could not deflect and instead of the peace he sought, he tormentedly confronted good and evil.

Learning to accept the one and reject the other, a spiritual path opened which revealed success beyond his wildest dreams. Suddenly, every conflict in life resolved itself. His broken heart healed as well as those of his loved ones. Learning the art of service, against which the serpent has no power, Ron became a man who makes a difference.

In *Wild Card* you will find your own spiritual path. Choose it. Change your life.

Printed in the United States
219478BV00004B/20/P

9 780976 112273